T0394778

FIRST WORDS IN...
Japanese

にほんご

ほん

おとうさん

おかあさん

しょくぶつ

by Kirsten Chang

BELLWETHER MEDIA • MINNEAPOLIS, MN

Blastoff! Readers are carefully developed by literacy experts to build reading stamina and move students toward fluency by combining standards-based content with developmentally appropriate text.

Level 1 provides the most support through repetition of high-frequency words, light text, predictable sentence patterns, and strong visual support.

Level 2 offers early readers a bit more challenge through varied sentences, increased text load, and text-supportive special features.

Level 3 advances early-fluent readers toward fluency through increased text load, less reliance on photos, advancing concepts, longer sentences, and more complex special features.

★ **Blastoff! Universe**

Reading Level

Grade **K**

Grades **1–3**

Grade **4**

This edition first published in 2026 by Bellwether Media, Inc.

No part of this publication may be reproduced in whole or in part without written permission of the publisher. For information regarding permission, write to Bellwether Media, Inc., Attention: Permissions Department, 3500 American Blvd W, Suite 150, Bloomington, MN 55431.

Library of Congress Cataloging-in-Publication Data

LC record for Japanese available at: https://lccn.loc.gov/2025019036

Editor: Suzane Nguyen   Designer: Andrea Schneider

Printed in the United States of America, North Mankato, MN.

tokei

Table of Contents

Konnichiwa!
I'm Kenji. Let's learn
some Japanese,
or *Nihongo* words.

konnichiwa
(KOHN-NEE-chee-wah)
hello

Words to Know

- はい .... hai (HI) ....yes
- いいえ .... iie (EE-yeh)........................ no
- にほんご .... Nihongo (nee-HON-goh).........
....Japanese
- おねがいします..onegaishimasu ....
(oh-neh-GUY-she-MAHS)....................please
- ありがとうございます..arigatou gozaimasu
(ar-ee-GOT-toh goh-ZAI-mahs)...................
....thank you
- すみません.... sumimasen...............................
(soo-mee-mah-SEN) ....excuse me

5

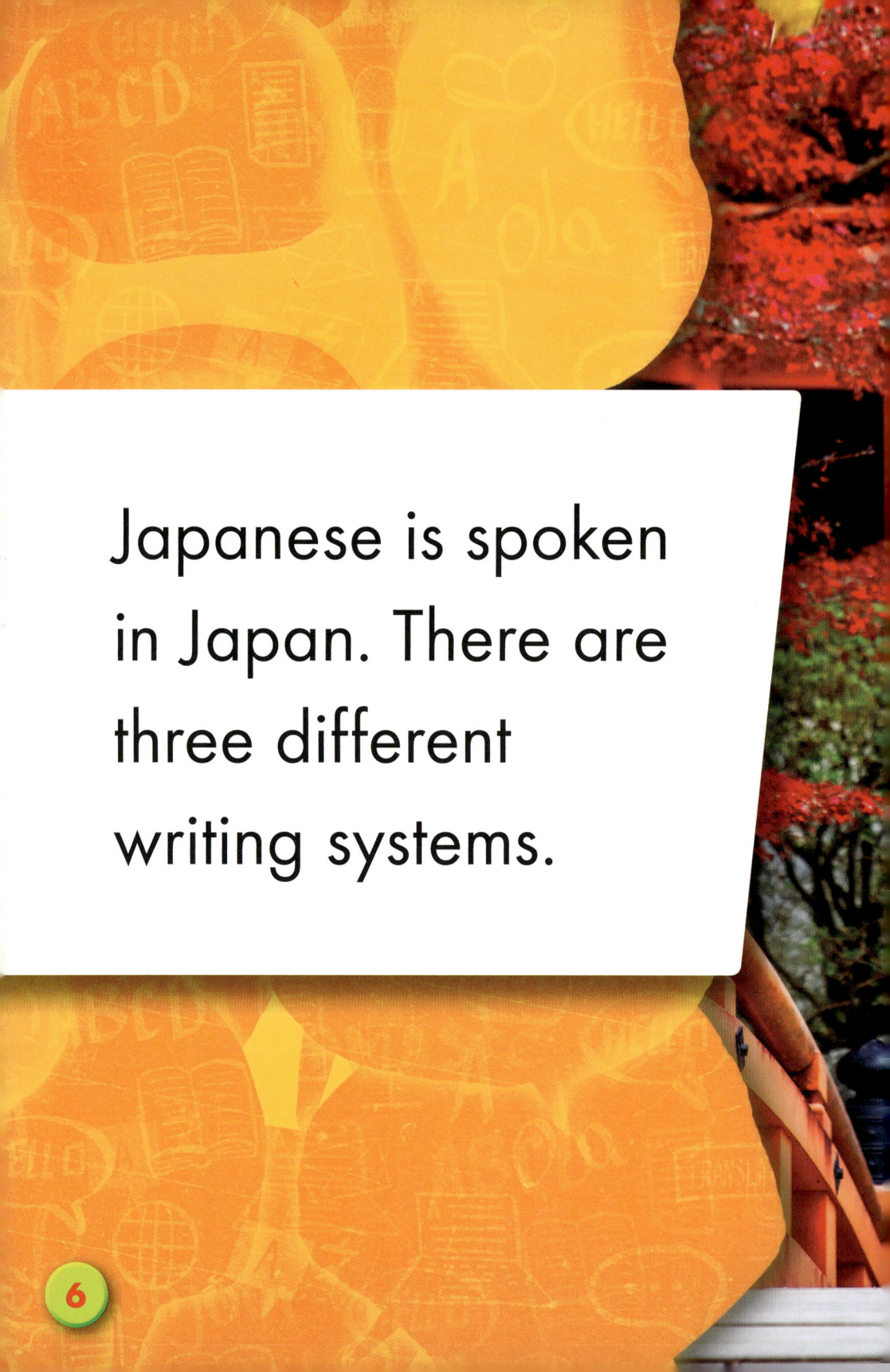

Japanese is spoken in Japan. There are three different writing systems.

6

Japanese-speaking Country

Japan

At Home

Ren lives with his *kazoku*. They live in an *ie*. They have an *inu*!

Words to Know

- おかあさん..okaasan (oh-KAH-san)..mother
- おとうさん..otousan (oh-TOH-san)....father
- いえ............ie (ee-AY)............................house
- かぞく.......kazoku (KAH-zoh-koo)..family
- いぬ............inu (EE-nuu)........................dog
- しょくぶつ..
  shokubutsu (show-KOO-boot-zoo)......plant

okaasan

otousan

inu

In the *asa*, Nami eats *asagohan*. **Miso soup** and vegetables are tasty.

miso soup

Words to Know

- あさ ....asa (AH-sah)...............**morning**
- あさごはん... asagohan (ah-SAH-goh-han) ....**breakfast**
- しるわん...shiruwan (SHE-roo-wan) ....**soup bowl**
- いす...........isu (ee-SOO).......................**chair**
- とけい.......tokei (toh-KAY)...............**clock**

shiruwan

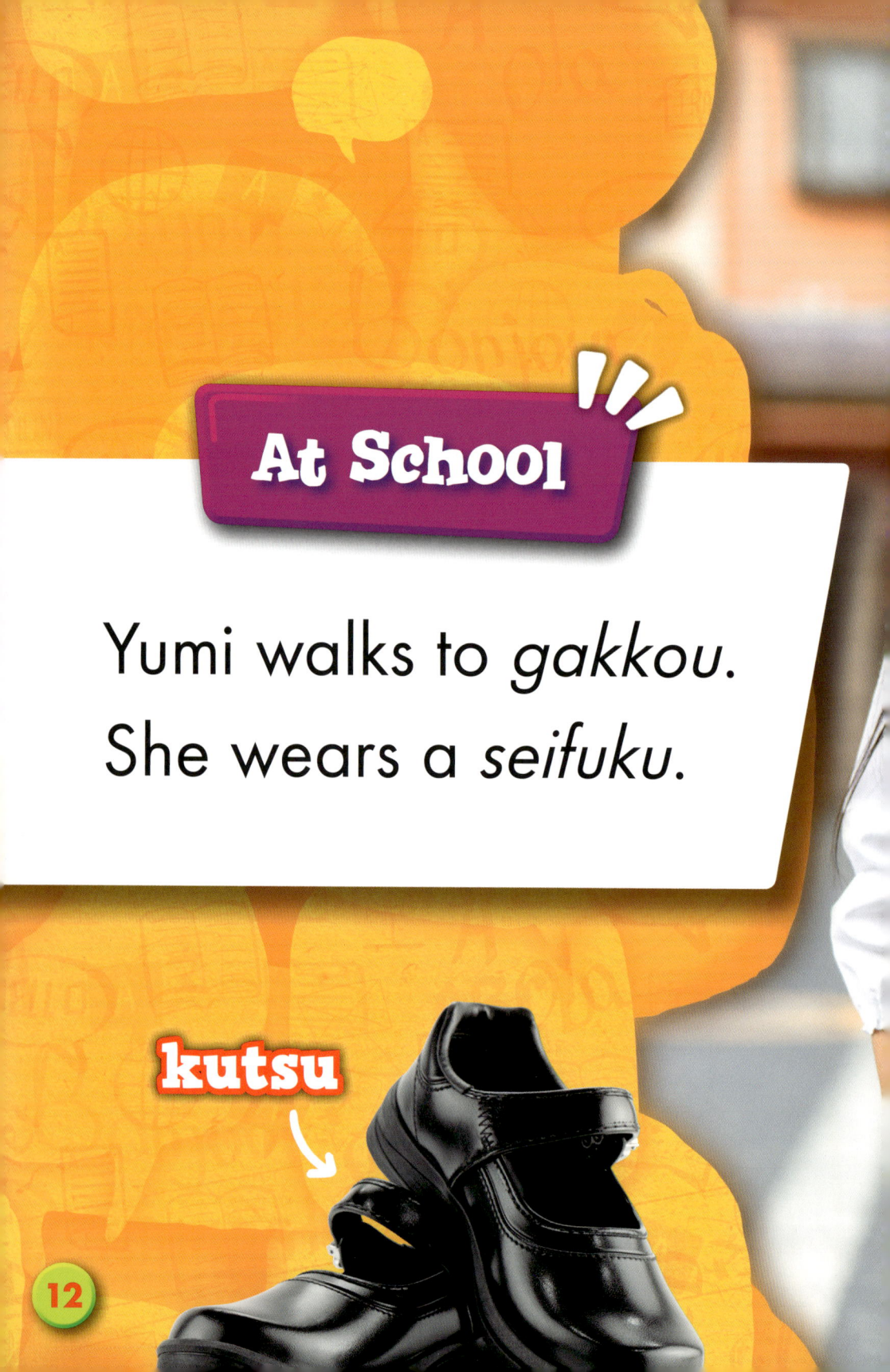

At School

Yumi walks to *gakkou*.
She wears a *seifuku*.

kutsu

Count in Japanese

いち	......ichi..	(EE-chee).....	1
に	..........ni.....	(NEE).....	2
さん	......san...	(SAHN).........	3
よん	......yon...	(YOHN)....	4
ご	..........go.....	(GO)....	5
ろく	......roku..	(ro-KOO)...	6
なな	......nana	(NAH-nah)......	7
はち	......hachi	(ha-CHEE)....	8
きゅう	..kyuu	(KYOO)....	9
じゅう	..juu....	(JOO).........	10

seifuku

Words to Know

- がっこう...gakkou (gah-KOH)..........school
- せいふく...seifuku (SAY-foo-koo)..uniform
- みち...........michi (me-CHEE)............street
- くつ............kutsu (koot-SU)................shoes

13

Gin practices writing in Japanese with an *enpitsu*. *Hon* are fun to read!

hon

14

Words to Know

- つくえ ......tsukue (su-KOO-ɑy) .... **desk**
- せんせい...sensei (sen-SAY)........... **teacher**
- きょうしつ ....
kyoushitsu (KYO-shee-zu) .... **classroom**
- えんぴつ...enpitsu (EN-peet-zu)...... **pencil**
- ほん...........hon (HOHN)..................... **books**

enpitsu

It is time to go to the *kouen*. Goro plays *yakyuu* with his *tomodachi*.

sakura

tama

tomodachi

Words to Know

- こうえん..... kouen (KOH-en)............**park**
- ともだち..... tomodachi ....
  (toh-moh-DAH-chee) ....**friends**
- やきゅう...... yakyuu (yah-KYOO)..............
  ....**baseball**
- たま............. tama (tah-MAH) ....**ball**
- はる............. haru (HA-roo) ....**spring**
- さくら......... sakura (sah-KOO-rah) ....
  .... **cherry blossoms**

Kiya eats *yorugohan*.
She uses her *hashi*.

onigiri

18

hashi

Words to Know

- よるごはん‥**yorugohan** (yo-roo-GOH-hahn) ....**dinner**
- はし...........**hashi** (HA-shee) ......**chopsticks**
- おさら ....**osara** (oh-sah-RAH) ....**plate**
- おにぎり .....**onigiri** (oh-nee-GEE-ree) ....**rice ball**
- みず............**mizu** (mee-ZOO) ....**water**

19

Kimi does *shukudai* before bed. It is time to sleep on the **futon**. *Oyasumi*!

oyasumi
(oh-YA-soo-mee)
good night

Words to Know

- しゅくだい.. shukudai (shoo-koo-DAI) ....
  ....homework
- ふとん.......... futon (foo-TOHN)...........
  ....mattress/bed
- かけぶとん ....
  kakebuton (kah-KAY-boo-TOHN) ....
  ....Japanese quilt
- まくら .... makura (MAH-koo-rah).......
  ....pillow
- じゃね.......... Jaa ne (JAH-neh)............
  ....bye/see you

21

Glossary

futon

a Japanese bed that is on the floor

miso soup

a type of soup made from a vegetable called a soybean

To Learn More

AT THE LIBRARY

Cacciapuoti, Aurora. *Let's Learn Japanese: First Words for Everyone*. San Francisco, Calif.: Chronicle Books, 2019.

Davis, Bela. *Intro to Japanese = Nihongo (ni·ho·n·go)*. Minneapolis, Minn.: Abdo Kids Junior, 2024.

Sabelko, Rebecca. *Japan*. Minneapolis, Minn.: Bellwether Media, 2023.

ON THE WEB

FACTSURFER

Factsurfer.com gives you a safe, fun way to find more information.

1. Go to www.factsurfer.com.

2. Enter "Japanese" into the search box and click 🔍.

3. Select your book cover to see a list of related content.

Index

bed, 20
count in
  Japanese, 13
eats, 10, 18
futon, 20
good night, 21
hello, 5
home, 8
Japan, 6
learn, 4
map, 7
miso soup, 10
plays, 16
read, 14
school, 12, 14

sleep, 20
words to know, 5,
  9, 11, 13, 15,
  17, 19, 21
writing systems, 6